D1159646

GRAMMAR BASICS

VERBS
KATE RIGGS

CREATIVE ● EDUCATION

Published by Creative Education
P.O. Box 227, Mankato, Minnesota 56002
Creative Education is an imprint of The Creative Company
www.thecreativecompany.us

Design and production by Liddy Walseth
Art direction by Rita Marshall
Printed in the United States of America

Photographs by Corbis (Hulton-Deutsch Collection), Getty Images (Maggie Duvall, Tim Flach,
GK Hart/Vikki Hart, Jessie Jean, John Lee, Roine Magnusson, Newspix, Maarten Wouters,
Jerry Young), iStockphoto (Matthew Dixon, fotoVoyager, Hedda Gjerpen, Eric Isselée, narvikk,
Natalia Sinjushina, Anett Somogyvári)

Library of Congress Cataloging-in-Publication Data
Riggs, Kate.
Verbs / by Kate Riggs.
p. cm. — (Grammar basics)
Summary: A simple overview of verbs—the words that tell what subjects do—including their uses
in sentences, their tenses and person, and how to match them with singular and plural nouns.
Includes bibliographical references and index.
ISBN 978-1-60818-239-8
1. English language—Verb—Juvenile literature. I. Title.
PE1271.R57 2013
428.2—dc23   2011050690

2 4 6 8 9 7 5 3

TABLE OF CONTENTS

INTRODUCTION

What do you *do* at school? You *talk* to friends. You *play* on the playground. You *listen* to your teachers. You *eat* your lunch. You *are* busy! All of these activities are verbs.

WHAT ARE VERBS?

The bus *drove* down the street.

A verb is an action or a state of being. It tells what words called **subjects** do. The subject of a **sentence** is a noun. Nouns are people, places, and things.

VERBS
IN USE

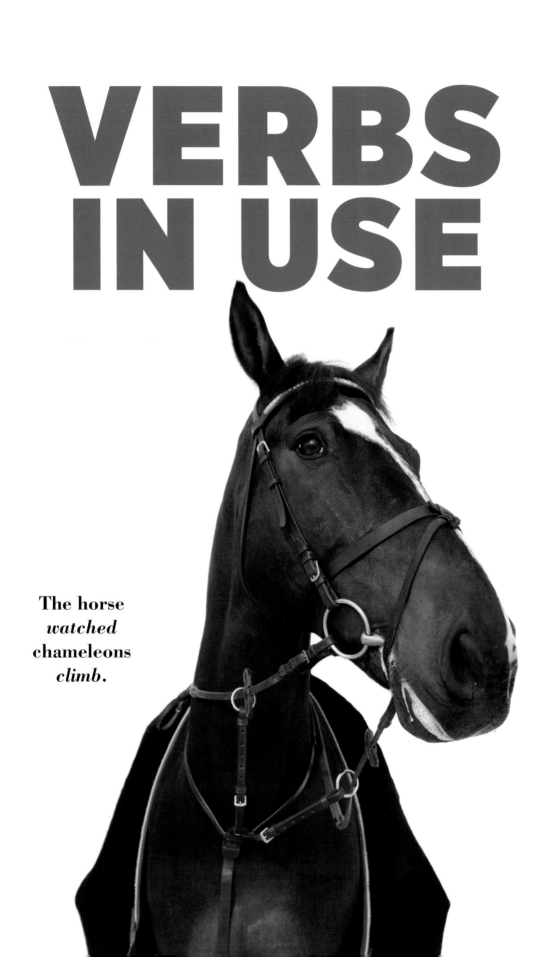

The horse *watched* chameleons *climb*.

Every sentence needs at least one main verb and one noun. Sometimes the main verb *is* a linking verb. Linking verbs such as *is* do not show action. They just *are*.

TENSING UP

My dog *helps* me *do* my homework.

Verbs can be in the present, past, or future tense. A present verb says what something *does* now. A past verb says what something *did* before. A future verb says what something *will do* later.

SPELLING CLUES

Many past verbs end in
–*ed*. You can tell that
something has **happened**
when you see –*ed*. Other
past verbs are spelled
differently. These are called
irregular verbs. **Do** is an
irregular verb. It can be **do**
or **does** in the present tense.
But its past tense is **did**.

LET'S GET PERSONAL

A verb can be in what is called "person," too. There are first-person (I, we), second-person (you), and third-person (he, she, it, they) verbs. The verb *be* becomes *am*, *is*, or *are* in the present tense. It takes the form of *was* or *were* in the past. Can you tell which sentence below is present and which one is past?

I *am* happy my birthday *is* today!

Mary and Laura *were* sad when the movie *ended*.

The dogs *wore* hats for the birthday party.

MATCHING GAME

The lioness *is looking* for her four cubs.

A verb has to match the person of a noun. Look back at the page you just read. Do you know why "I am" is right? *Am* is the form of *be* that goes with first-person, **singular** nouns like "I." You would not say "I is" or "I are," would you?

PLURAL PAIRS

Verbs that go with **plural** nouns have to be plural, too. In the first person, "we" is a plural noun. If you wanted to use a form of *be* as your verb, what would go with "we"?

We *are* sitting quietly. We *were* making a lot of noise.

We *saw*
peacocks
and vultures
at the zoo.

LOOK OUT FOR VERBS!

Verbs are the actions that make up our lives. You *wake* in the morning. You *eat* meals. You *read* books. No matter what you *do*, you will always need a verb!

The brothers *ate* their breakfast before school.

GRAMMAR GAME TIME

Have you ever played Simon Says? In this game, one person is Simon, or the leader. Everyone else has to do what Simon says—but only when they hear the words "Simon says" first! If the leader does not say, "Simon says," don't do the action! Use the verbs you know to play with a few friends. Start by saying, "Simon says, walk in place." Simon might also say to *jump, clap, stomp,* or *stand* still. Keep playing until Simon says to stop!

GRAMMAR WORD BANK

plural—more than one

sentence—a group of words that has a noun as the subject and a verb

singular—one of something

subjects—the nouns that are what or whom sentences are about

READ MORE

Fleming, Maria. *Grammar Tales: A Verb for Herb*. New York: Scholastic, 2004.

Heller, Ruth. *Kites Sail High: A Book about Verbs*. New York: Grosset & Dunlap, 1988.

WEB SITES

Grammar Blast

http://www.eduplace.com/kids/hme/k_5/grammar/

Test your verb knowledge by taking the quiz at your grade level.

Grammar Ninja

http://www.kwarp.com/portfolio/grammarninja.html

Beginner ninjas can find the verbs (and nouns) in each sentence.

INDEX